CLIFF RICHARD

HIS GREATEST HITS

PIANO VOCAL GUITAR

© International Music Publications Ltd
First published in 2001 by International Music Publications Ltd
International Music Publications Ltd is a Faber Music company
3 Queen Square, London WC1N 3AU
Editor: Anna Joyce   Folio Design: Dominic Brookman
Printed in England by Caligraving Ltd
All rights reserved.
ISBN10: 0-571-53084-2   EAN13: 978-0-571-53084-7

BACHELOR BOY

Words and Music by
BRUCE WELCH AND CLIFF RICHARD

1. When I was young___ my fa - ther said "Son I have
2. When I was six - teen I fell___ in love with a girl___ as

some - thing to say."___ And what he told me I'll
sweet as can be.___ But I re - mem - bered

Can't Keep This Feeling In

Words and Music by
ARNOLD ROMAN, STEVE SKINNER
and DENNIS LAMBERT

CARRIE

Words and Music by
TERRY BRITTEN and B.A. ROBERTSON

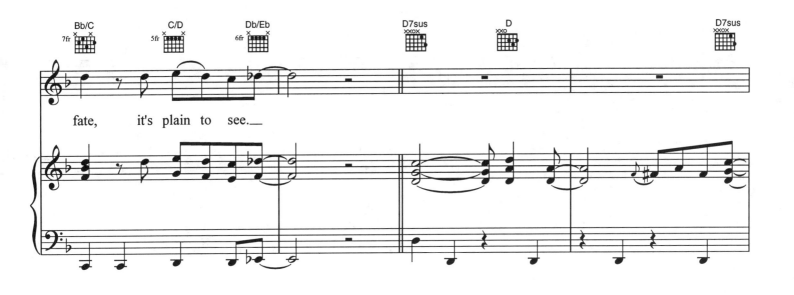

fate, it's plain to see.___

An-oth-er miss-ing per - son,

one of ma - ny, we as - sume._____ The young wear their free

- dom like cheap_ per - fume.

(It's use - less in - for - ma - tion) re - turn - ing my call.__ (To help the sit - u -

a - tion) they've noth - ing at all._____ You're just an - oth - er mes - sage on a pay phone

DO YOU WANNA DANCE

Words and Music by
ROBERT FREEMAN

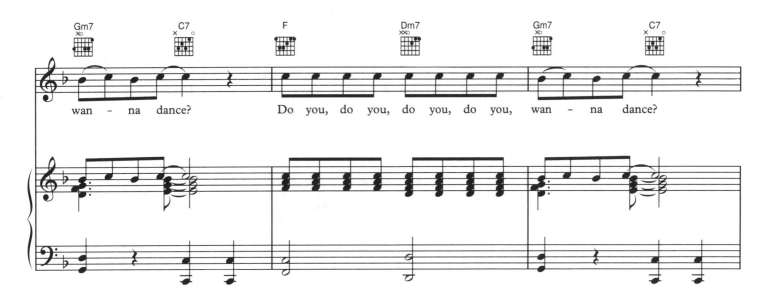

wan - na dance? Do you, do you, do you, do you, wan - na dance?

Do you, do you, do you, do you want___ to___ dance?_____

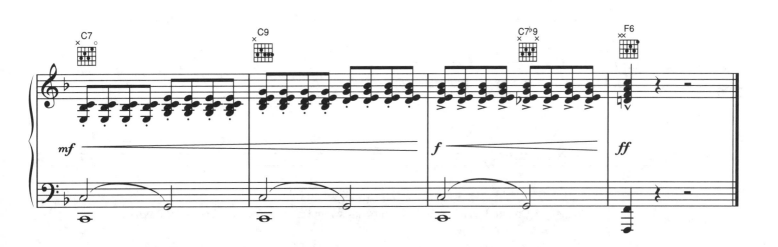

DADDY'S HOME

Words and Music by
JAMES SHEPPARD
and WILLIAM MILLER

Very slow

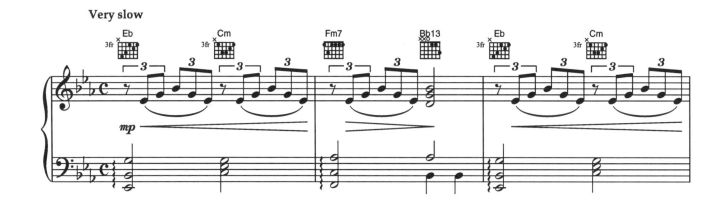

You're my love,___ you're my an - gel,___ you're the girl___ of my dreams.

I'd like to thank you_ for_ wait - ing_ pa - tient - ly. Dad - dy's home,

Campbell Connelly & Co Ltd, London W1V 5TZ and Windswept Pacific Music Ltd, London W6 9BD

DEVIL WOMAN

Words and Music by
TERRY BRITTEN
and CHRISTINE HOLMES

She's just a dev - il wo - man   with e - vil on her mind._   Be - ware the dev - il wo - man,

she's gon - na get you!   She's just a dev - il wom - an   with e - vil on her mind._

Be - ware the dev - il wo - man,   she's gon - na get you from be - hind!

care - ful of the neigh - bour - hood strays,___ of a la - dy with long__

__ black hair___ try - in' to win you with her fem - i - nine ways.___

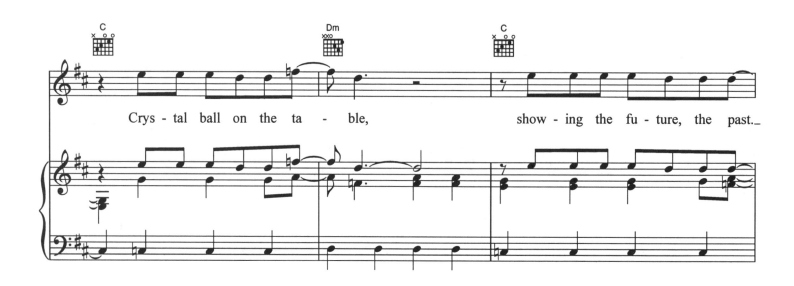

Crys - tal ball on the ta - ble, show - ing the fu - ture, the past.__

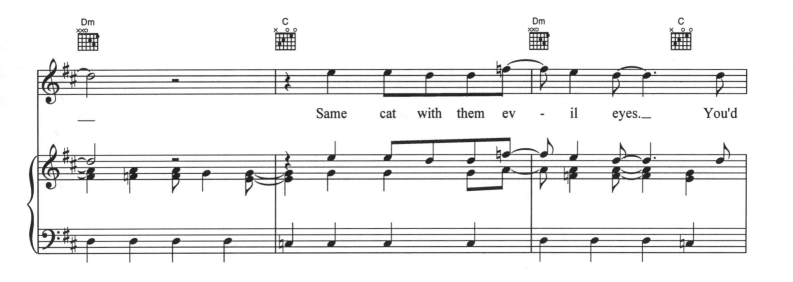

Same cat with them ev - il eyes.__ You'd

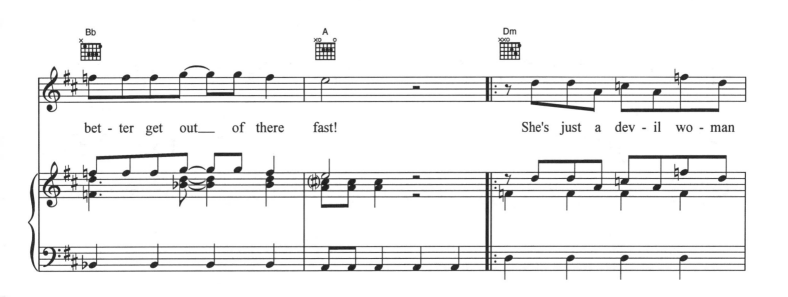

bet - ter get out__ of there fast! She's just a dev - il wo - man

repeat and fade

with ev - il on her mind.__ Be - ware the dev - il wo - man, she's gon - na get you!

repeat and fade

DREAMIN'

Words and Music by
ALAN TARNEY and LEO SAYER

Medium beat

Four o' clock, I've been walk - in' all __ night, it's the time __ I al - ways think __ of __
life.) Five o' clock, __ still walk - in' a round, _____ I call you up, but you just bring me

you. If you could on - ly see __ through my __ eyes
down. I guess you'd say I'm get - ting no - where

then you'd know just __ what __ I'm go - in' through. __
but in my dreams you al - ways come __ a - round. __

FROM A DISTANCE

Words and Music by
JULIE GOLD

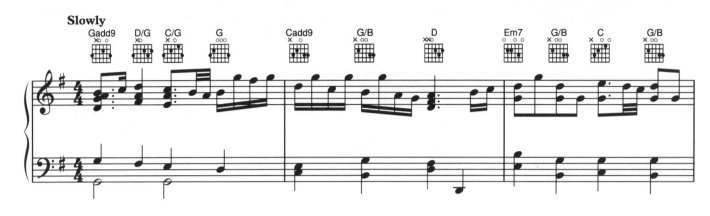

From a dis-tance, the world looks blue___ and green,___ and the
(see additional lyrics)

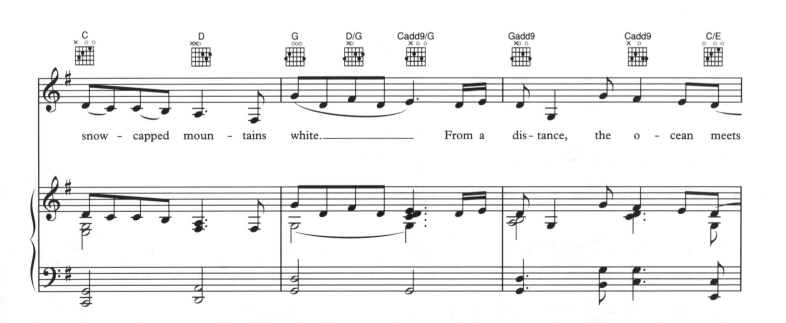

snow - capped moun - tains white.___ From a dis - tance, the o - cean meets

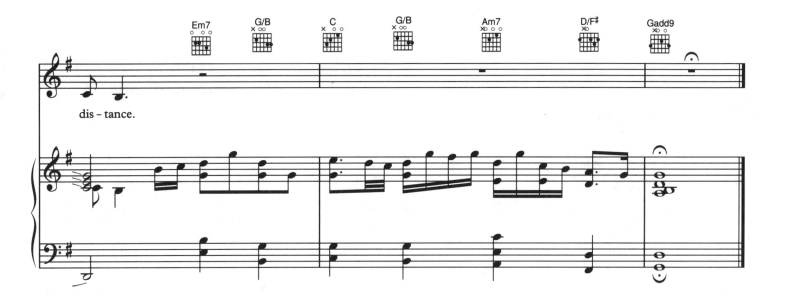

dis – tance.

Verse 2:
From a distance, we all have enough
And no one is in need
There are no guns, no bombs, no diseases
No hungry mouths to feed
From a distance, we are instruments
Marching in a common band
Playing songs of hope, playing songs of peace
They're the songs of every man

Verse 3:
From a distance, you look like my friend
Even though we are at war
From a distance I just cannot comprehend
What all this fighting is for
From a distance there is harmony
And it echoes through the land
It's the hope of hopes, it's the love of loves
It's the heart of every man

IT'S ALL IN THE GAME

Words and Music by
CHARLES DAWES
and CARL SIGMAN

41

LIVING DOLL

Words and Music by
LIONEL BART

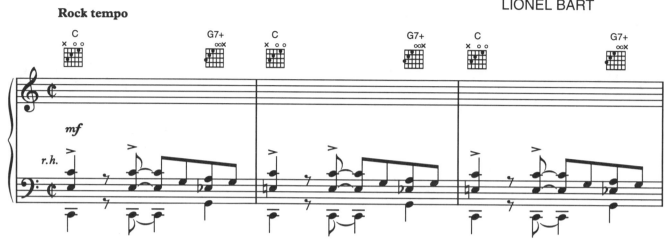

Got_ my-self a cry-ing, talk-ing, sleep-ing, walk-ing, liv-ing doll,_

_ got_ to do my best to please her, just 'cos she's a

liv - ing doll._____ Such_ a rov - ing eye, and that is

why she sat - is - - - fies my soul._____ Got_ the one an'

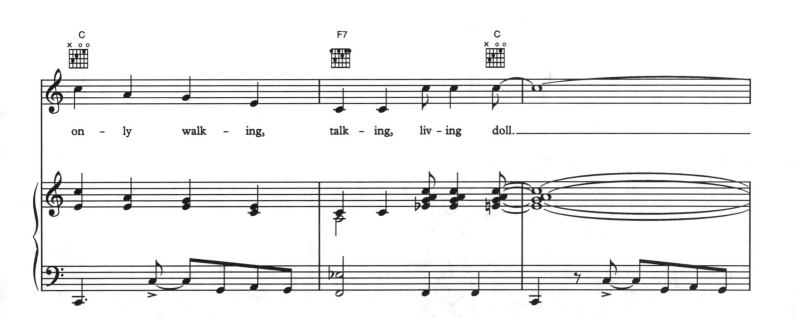

on - ly walk - ing, talk - ing, liv - ing doll._____

Take a look at her hair, it's real! And if you don't be-

lieve what I say___ just feel! I'm gon-na lock her up in a trunk___ so

no big hunk can steal her a-way___ from me.___ Got___ my-self a

MILLENNIUM PRAYER

Words and Music by
PAUL FIELD and STEPHEN DEAL

Our Fa - - ther who— art in hea - ven, hal - lowed be Thy— name. Thy— king - dom come, Thy— will be done on— earth— as in

THE MINUTE YOU'RE GONE

Words and Music by
JIMMY GATELEY

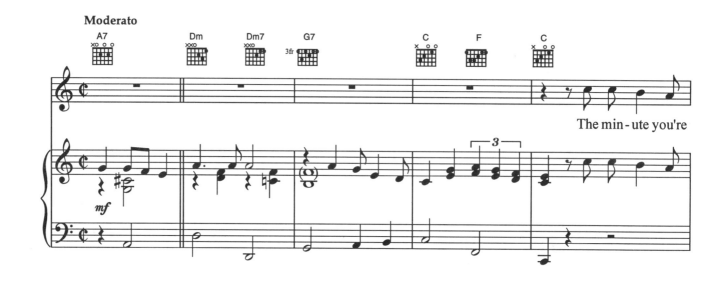

oh, so blue, If I could-n't be with you. The min - ute you're gone, I pray,

the min - ute you're gone I say, please don't stay a - way too long

the min - ute you're gone. The min - ute you're gone.

MISTLETOE AND WINE

Words and Music by
KEITH STRACHAN, JEREMY PAUL
and LESLIE STEWART

Easy relaxed tempo

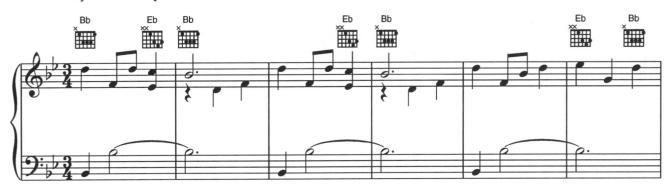

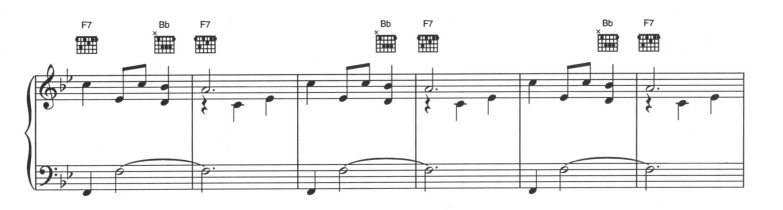

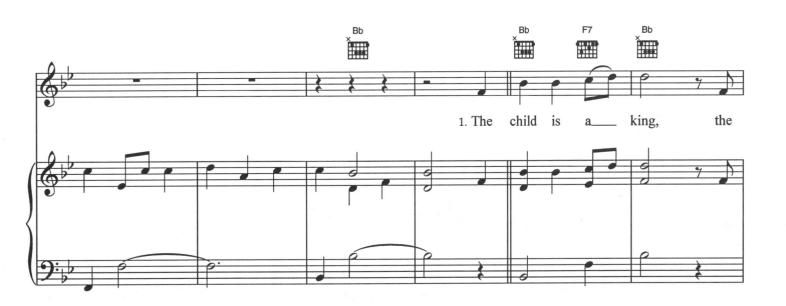

1. The child is a___ king, the

car - oll - ers__ sing, the old is passed, there's a new_____ be - gin - ning.

Dreams of San - ta, dreams of snow, fin - gers numb,

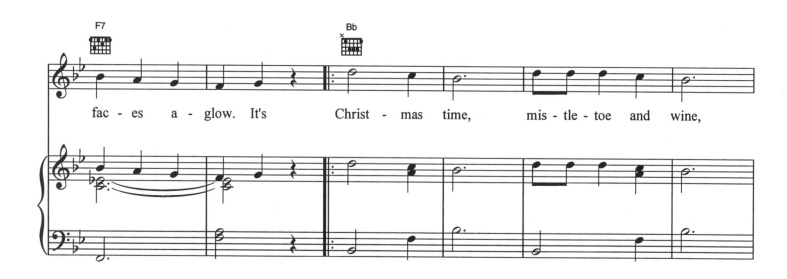

fac - es a - glow. It's Christ - mas time, mis - tle - toe and wine,

child - ren sing - ing Chris - ti - an rhyme with logs on the fire___ and

gifts on the tree; A time to re - joice in the good that we

see. 2. A time___ for liv - ing, a time for be - liev - ing, a
3. It's a time___ for giv - ing, a time for get - ting, a

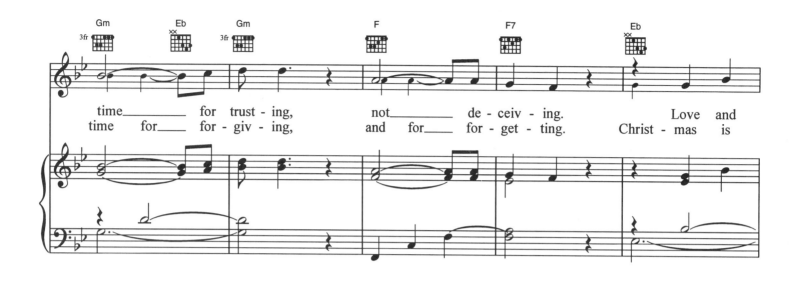

time____ for trust - ing, not____ de - ceiv - ing. Love and
time for____ for - giv - ing, and for____ for - get - ting. Christ - mas is

laugh - ter and joy ev - er af - ter Ours for the tak - ing just
love,____ Christ - mas is peace; A time____ for hat - ing____ and

fol - low____ the mas - ter. cease. Christ - mas time,
fight - ing____ to

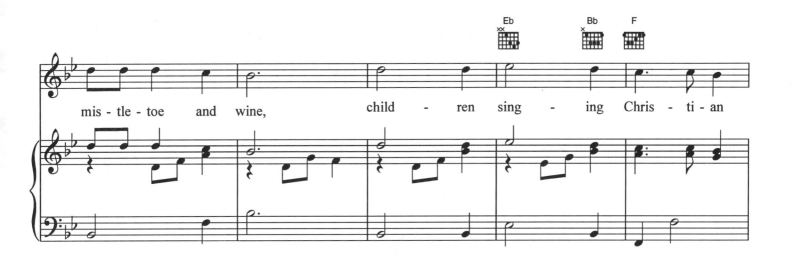

mis - tle - toe and wine, child - ren sing - ing Chris - ti - an

rhyme with logs on the fire___ and gifts on the tree; A

time to re - joice in the good that we see. see.

MOVE IT

Words and Music by
IAN SAMWELL

Come on pret - ty ba - by let's a - move it and a-groove it.

Yeah, let's shake oh, ba - by, shake, oh, hon - ey please don't lose _____ it.

move it.   Hey, hey, oh move it.   Uh-huh let's

MY PRETTY ONE

Words and Music by
ALAN TARNEY

1. Well I've dreamed a - bout to - day,___ the same dream in
2. Well I've dreamed a - bout to - day,___ the same dream in so

THE NEXT TIME

Words and Music by
BUDDY KAYE and PHILIP SPRINGER

some - one else will mend the heart you've bro - ken _____ in ____ two. _____

____ But how can I fall ____ in love the

next time, when I'm still so ve - ry much in

THE ONLY WAY OUT

Words and Music by
RAY MARTINEZ

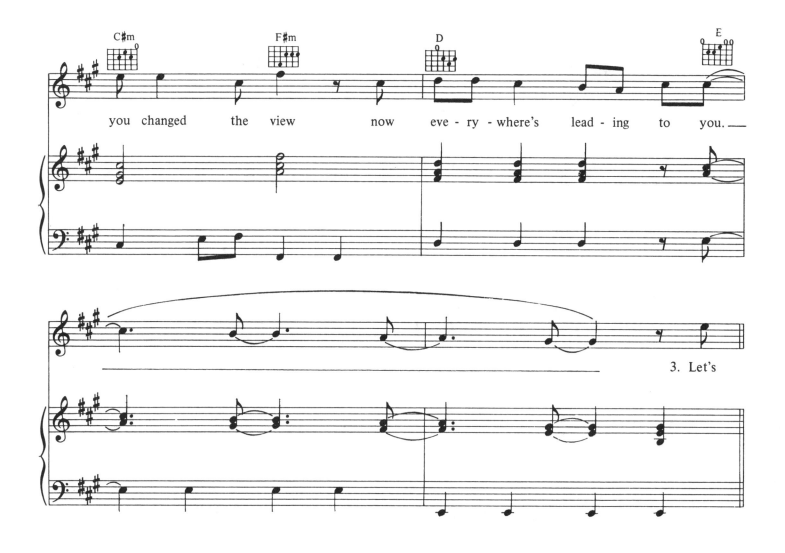

you changed the view now eve - ry - where's lead - ing to you.

3. Let's

VERSE 3: Let's get this thing going let's move it along
          Let me do all the things I've been missing so long.
          'Cause the only way out is the only way in and it's you.

VERSE: (Instr.)

MIDDLE: I spent a lot of time at the crossroads
          Getting that lonely feeling inside
          Suddenly you made the rescue you pulled me through
          Now let me do something for you.

          (Link chords: E/F♯)

[KEY: B]

VERSE 4: Let's get this thing going let's move it along
          Let's do all the things I've been missing so long.
          And the only way out is the only way in and it's you,
          Yeah the only way out is the only way in and it's you,
          Yeah the only way out is the only way in and it's you.

INTRO: (Repeat) + The only way out
                      It's the only way in
                      It's the only way out
                      It's the only way in . . . . .
                                        (FADE)

PEACE IN OUR TIME

Words and Music by
PETE SINFIELD and ANDY HILL

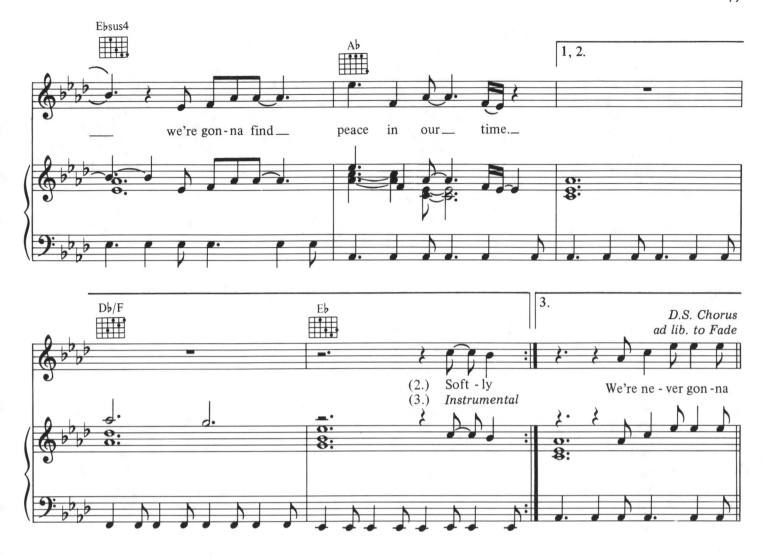

VERSE 2:
Softly softly,
When there is lightning in the sky;
When the rivers are rising
And trouble rolls in on the tide.
We'll keep on keeping on
Till all the tears are dry;
We'll weather the storm and welcome the dawn
Of tomorrow, you and I.
We've gotta have faith and get it fast;
Faith and hope, make it last;
Give us strength to reach the stars;
Put a song in our hearts.

VERSE 3:

INSTRUMENTAL — 12 BARS

We're raising the dust, it's heaven or bust
And we'll see this dream come true.
We're gonna have faith *(faith)*, the road will be long;
But there's hope *(hope)* to carry on;
We'll have strength *(strength)*; we'll never go wrong
With this song in our hearts.

PLEASE DON'T FALL IN LOVE

Words and Music by
MIKE BATT

Please don't fall in love. I

know you don't tell—— me To spare me the pain,—— Don't want you to tell—— me, I

don't need his name,—— But I'm beg-ging you, Ba——by, Please don't fall in——

love.

PLEASE DON'T TEASE

Words and Music by
BRUCE WELCH and PETE CHESTER

won't.____ You love me like a hur-ri cane,_ and then you start to

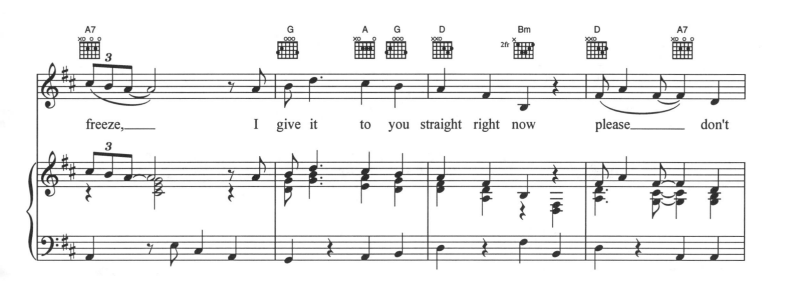

freeze,____ I give it to you straight right now please____ don't

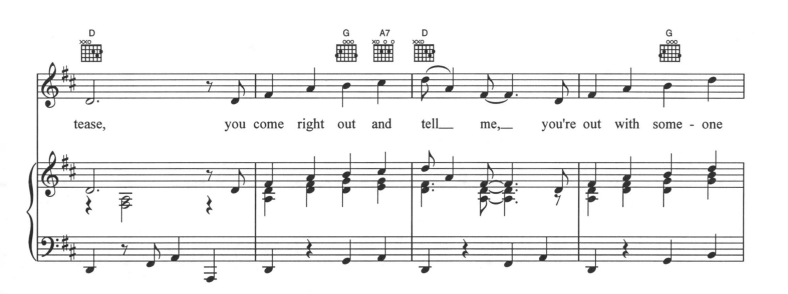

tease, you come right out and tell_ me,_ you're out with some - one

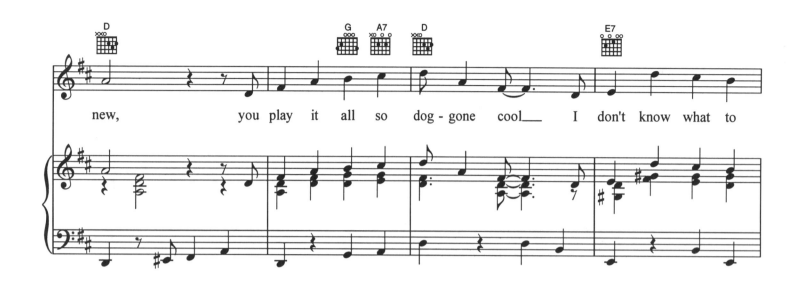

new,   you play it all so dog - gone cool___ I don't know what to

do._____   You nev - er seem to an - swer me___ you just don't hear my

plea,_____   I'll give it to you one more time,   please_____ don't

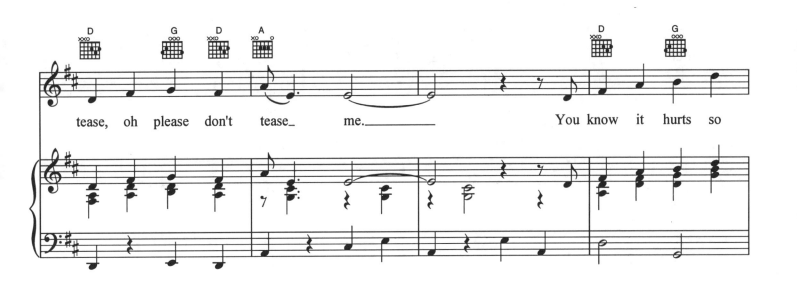

tease, oh please don't tease_ me._____ You know it hurts so

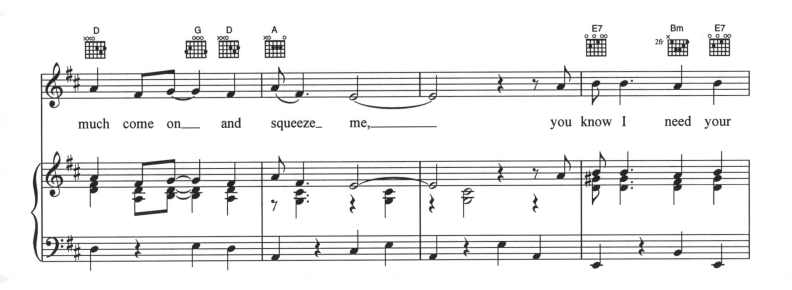

much come on__ and squeeze_ me,_____ you know I need your

ten - der touch, but you tell me that you love me ba - by, then you say you don't,_

SHE'S SO BEAUTIFUL

Words and Music by
HANS POULSEN

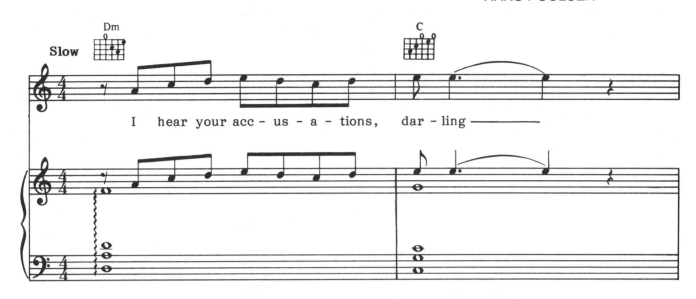

Moderate beat

River flow to shin— ing sea,— Mount-ain bit— ter blue;—
Ti- ny plan- et spins—through space,— Gives my life— to me,—

Child-ren flow like wa — ter falls,— Sweet our love— re-new.—
Fif-teen bill - ion hu— man beings— Where's our des - tin - y?—

Peace and war and peace— a - gain,—

SOME PEOPLE

Words and Music by
ALAN TARNEY

SUMMER HOLIDAY

Words and Music by
BRUCE WELCH and BRIAN BENNETT

Capo 3

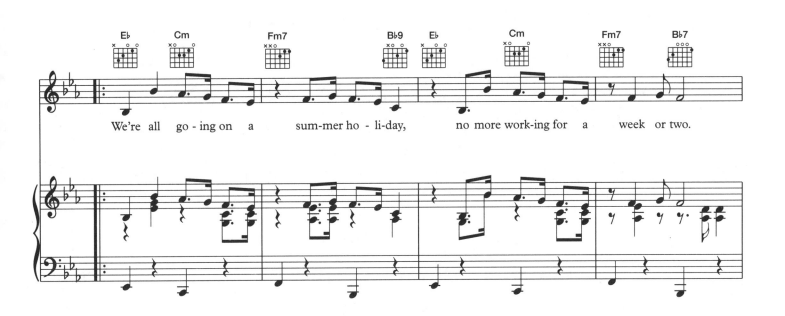

We're all go-ing on a sum-mer ho-li-day, no more work-ing for a week or two.

Fun and laugh-ter on our sum-mer ho-li-day, no more_ wor-ries for me or you,

TRAVELLIN' LIGHT

Words and Music by
SID TEPPER and ROY C BENNETT

hoot and a hol-ler a - way from pa - ra - dise._____ Tra-vel-in'

light,_____ tra-vel-in' light._____ I just can't wait to

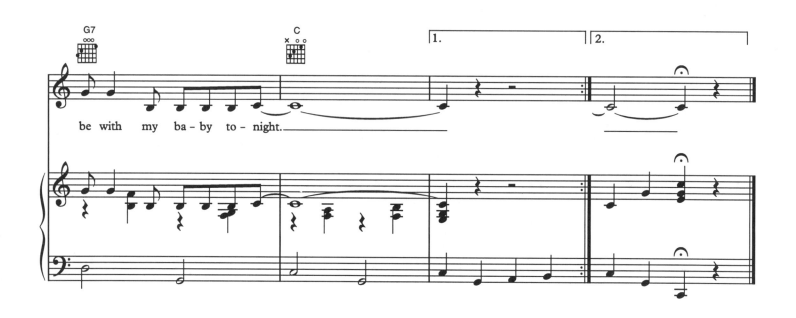

be with my ba-by to-night._____

TRUE LOVE WAYS

Words and Music by
BUDDY HOLLY and NORMAN PETTY

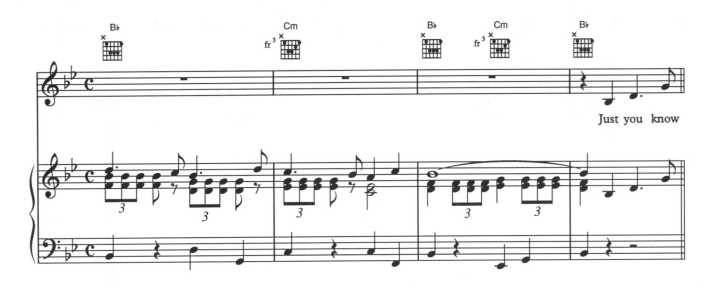

Just you know

why,   why you   and   I   will   by   and

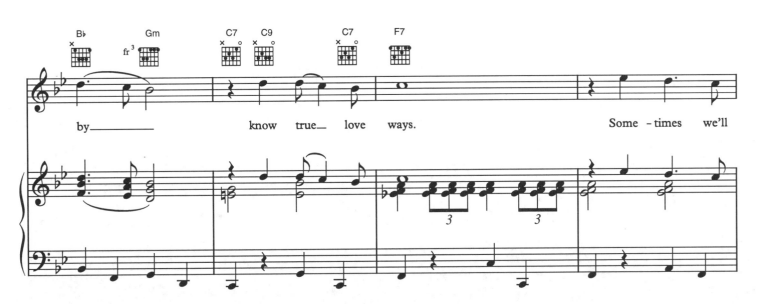

by_____   know true___ love   ways.   Some - times   we'll

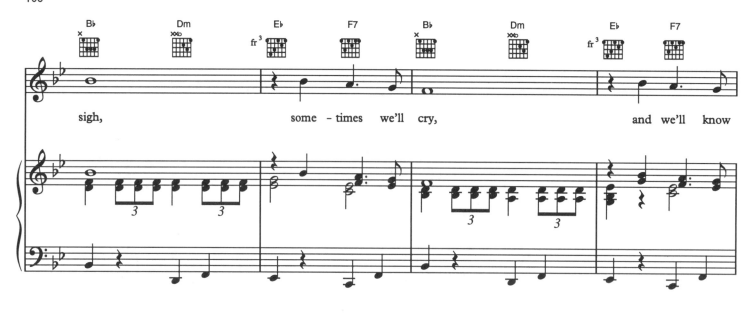

sigh,   some – times we'll cry,   and we'll know

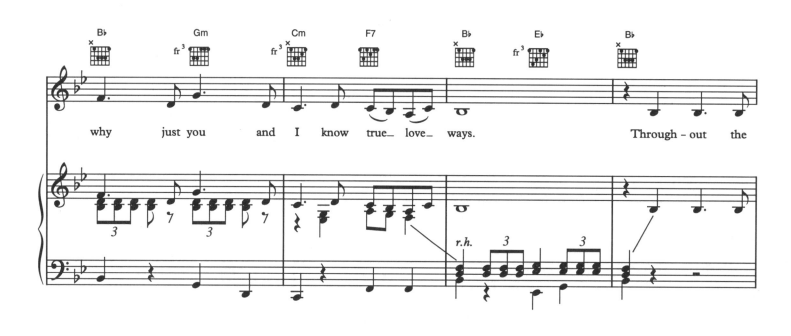

why   just you   and I know true_ love_ ways.   Through – out the

days   our true love ways   will bring us

WE DON'T TALK ANYMORE

Words and Music by
ALAN TARNEY

110

WIRED FOR SOUND

Words and Music by
B.A. ROBERTSON
and ALAN TARNEY

now, it's mus - ic___ I've found___ and I'm wir - ed___ for

sound._____

I___ like small speak - ers, I___ like tall speak - ers.

If___ they've mus - ic___ they're wir - ed___ for sound.

To Coda ⊕

D.%. (with repeat)
al Coda

⊕ *CODA*

(Repeat to Fade)

THE YOUNG ONES

Words and Music by
ROY BENNETT and SID TEPPER

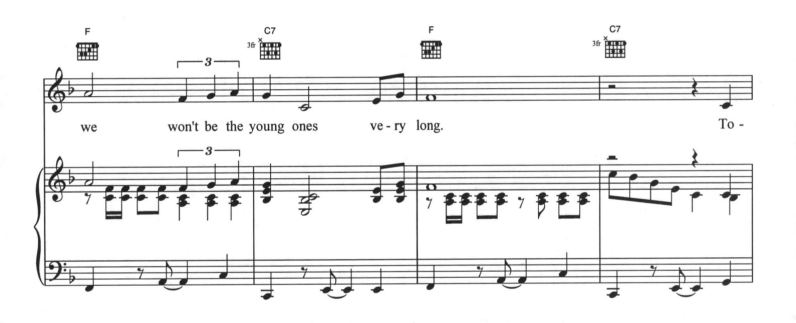

mor - row_ some - times ne - ver comes. So

love, me, there's a song to be sung and the

best time is to sing it while we're young.

Once in ev - 'ry life - time   comes a love like this.

I   need you   and you   need me,   oh my darl - ing can't you   see____

young_ dreams_   should be dreamed to - geth - er,_

young_ hearts,_ should-n't be a-fraid. And

some day, when the years_ have flown, darl - ing

this we'll teach the young ones of our own. The

own. The young ones, darl-ing we're the

young ones. The young ones

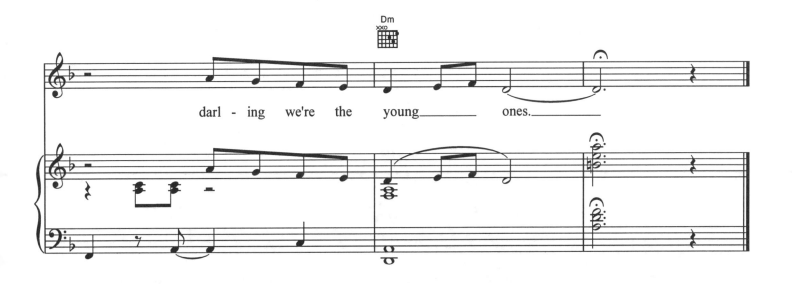

darl-ing we're the young ones.

YOU'RE THE VOICE

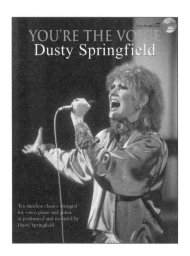
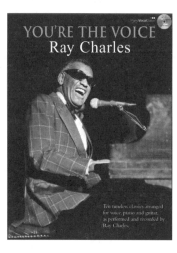
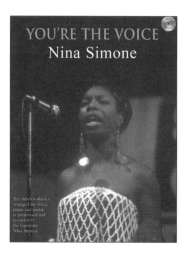

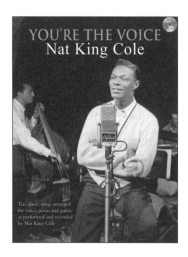
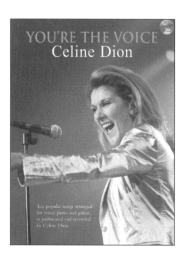
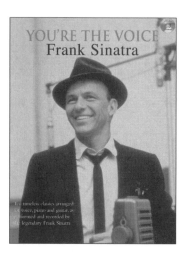

The outstanding vocal series from Faber Music
CD contains full backings for each song,
professionally arranged to recreate the sounds of the original recording

Shirley Bassey · Michael Bublé · Maria Callas · Eva Cassidy · Ray Charles
Nat King Cole · Sammy Davis Jr · Celine Dion · Aretha Franklin · Billie Holiday
Norah Jones · Tom Jones · Carole King · Madonna · George Michael
Dean Martin · Bette Midler · Matt Monro · Nina Simone
Frank Sinatra · Dusty Springfield · Barbra Streisand

FABER *ff* MUSIC

To buy Faber Music publications or to find out about the full range of titles available
please contact your local music retailer or Faber Music sales enquiries:

Faber Music Ltd, Burnt Mill, Elizabeth Way, Harlow CM20 2HX
Tel: +44 (0) 1279 82 89 82   Fax: +44 (0) 1279 82 89 83
sales@fabermusic.com   fabermusic.com   expressprintmusic.com